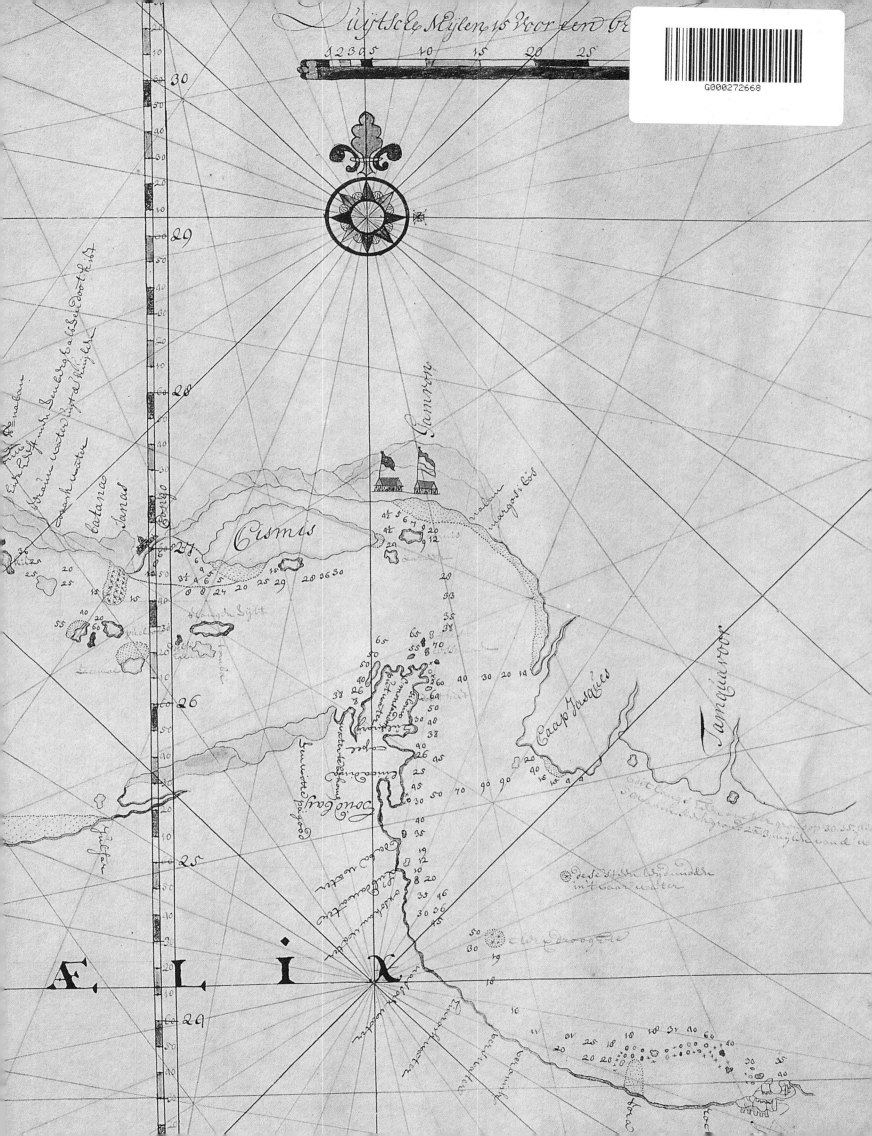

Now & Then
ABU DHABI

Above: His Highness Sheikh Zayed bin Sultan Al Nahyan with his sons in 2000.
Left: A portrait in oil of His Highness Sheikh Zayed bin Sultan Al Nahyan painted in 1970 in Al Ain by David Shepherd *OBE. FRSA. GAVA.*

Our Earth Series
Volume VII
Christine C. Nowell
& Nick Crawley

Foreword

From its humble beginnings, Abu Dhabi has gained a reputation on the world stage not only as an engine for economic progress, but also as a world centre for aviation, the associated aviation maintenance business, finance and the oil and gas industry.

Due largely to the foresight of H.H. Sheikh Zayed bin Sultan Al Nahyan when he took over as Ruler of Abu Dhabi in 1966, a most profound transformation has taken place throughout the emirate.

A vision that was cast back in 1971 with the formation of the United Arab Emirates has continued today with Abu Dhabi's growing reputation for international business and foreign investment.

With an ability to maintain a balance between progress as an international player shaping the 21st century and maintaining traditional Islamic values, Abu Dhabi's people and culture have endeared themselves to the world.

Contained within these pages is a photographic record of Abu Dhabi's achievements presented in a unique "Now & Then" way, the past compared with the present.

It is hoped that through the pages of this book you will experience what Abu Dhabi has to offer today, but more importantly you will understand and appreciate how Abu Dhabi started and the transformation that has taken place under the visionary leadership of Sheikh Zayed.

H.E. Sheikh Hamdan Bin Mubarak Al Nahyan
Chairman, Department of Civil Aviation.

Now & Then

ABU DHABI

ZODIAC PUBLISHING

Our Earth Series

Volume VII

Christine C. Nowell
& Nick Crawley

Published by Zodiac Publishing, Dubai.

Zodiac Publishing, Registered Office
P.O.Box 170, Churchill Buildings
Grand Turk, Turks & Caicos Islands

Zodiac Publishing, Dubai
PO Box 35121, Dubai, UAE
Tel: 0971 4 - 2826966 Fax: 0971 4 - 2826882
e-mail: zodiacpublishing@hotmail.com

First published 2001.

Copyright: Christine Nowell & Nick Crawley 2001.

Other books in the series:

 Now & Then The Emirates
 Now & Then Bahrain
 Now & Then Oman
 Now & Then Dubai

*A Day Above Oman
*A Day Above The Emirates
 A Day Above Yemen
 A Day Above Jiddah Island
* These books are published by Motivate Publishing

ISBN 0 - 9533033-4-9

British Library Cataloguing - in - Publication Data.
A catalogue record for this book is available
from the British Library.

Design by Nick Crawley of Zodiac Publishing.
Separations by Color Lines
Printing by Emirates Printing Press, Dubai.
"Now & Then" is a Zodiac Publishing registered trademark.

Contents

Page 6/7:
AN AERIAL VIEW OF ABU DHABI TAKEN IN 1954 shows the dramatic changes which have taken place in the last 50 years. At that time Al Hisn Fort was the largest building in the city and stood apart from all the other buildings. The first broad layouts of the road system can be seen, whilst just offshore, lighters ferry passengers, goods and vehicles across the shallow waters from freighters anchored more than four miles out to sea. These ferry passengers were some of the first visitors from abroad.

Page 8/9:
THIS PICTURE SHOWS H.H. SHEIKH ZAYED BIN Sultan AI Nahyan, President of the United Arab Emirates and Ruler of Abu Dhabi, seated in his informal majlis in the desert near AI Ain. In the past, such gatherings happened each evening to socialise, exchange news and information. During these gatherings anyone present could approach H.H. Sheikh Zayed to ask for advice about pressing matters. H.H. Sheikh Zayed has always had the deepest respect from his people who value his knowledge and wisdom.

This page:
FOR THOUSANDS OF YEARS THE CAMEL HAS PLAYED A fundamental role in the life of the people of Abu Dhabi. Camels are and always have been a self-contained means of existence for the nomadic tribes whose lives were spent in the never-ending search for adequate supplies of fresh water and good grazing for their animals. While the meat of slaughtered camels provided food, their milk provided much needed nourishment. This meat eked out the meagre food supplies, whilst the skin of the camel was made into clothes or tent coverings. Camels offer the most efficient and lasting means of transport in this arid desert climate. Camels can travel for many days without water and needing little food. More importantly for the nomads, camels were the means by which the tribesmen measured their wealth; the more camels a man had, the richer he was considered to be.

Introduction
by Peter Hellyer.

THE EARLIEST KNOWN INHABITANTS OF THE EMIRATE OF ABU DHABI LIVED IN THE INLAND AL AIN area and on the offshore islands over 7,000 years ago. The oldest site so far identified is on the island of Marawah, dating back to around 5,500 BC. While sites from this period have not been found on the island of Abu Dhabi itself, perhaps hidden as a result of recent development, there were certainly people living on and around the small hills that lie in the middle of the Abu Dhabi Airport Golf Club, since fine flint tools have been collected there.

Even closer to Abu Dhabi City, the island of Umm al-Nar, The Mother of Fire, home to the country's first oil refinery, was a port from around 2700 BC to 2200 BC, in the Bronze Age, exporting copper from the Hajar Mountains near Al Ain to the rising civilisations of Mesopotamia (present-day Iraq) and also trading with the Indus Valley.

By around 1000 BC, trading links had been established across the deserts of southern Arabia with Marib in Yemen, the land of the fabled Queen of Sheba, which grew wealthy for a thousand years or so on the proceeds of trade in frankincense. With the conversion of the Roman Emperors to Christianity, the demand for incense largely disappeared and Marib and its rivals vanished, their decline being hastened by the collapse of a great dam at Marib which permitted the irrigation of thousands of hectares of land.

Centuries before that, though, successive waves of migration from Yemen to the United Arab Emirates had begun. Among those to migrate along routes through Hadramaut and Oman and around the northern desert of Saudi Arabia and the Gulf coast were the ancestors of the Bani Yas tribal confederation, who came first to the Gulf coast of Abu Dhabi and then moved south to the Liwa Oasis. Today headed by President His Highness Sheikh Zayed bin Sultan Al Nahyan, the Bani Yas are the largest of the UAE's tribal groupings.

Modern research suggests that Homo sapiens (modern man), evolved around 200,000 years ago in East Africa. The ancient land bridges that existed before the emergence of the Red Sea and the Arabian Gulf, permitting animals from Africa to cross into Arabia and onwards into Asia, had vanished in the Miocene era, perhaps ten or so million years ago. Homo sapiens were still able, however, to spread up into the area of the Middle East, known to historians and archaeologists as the Fertile Crescent. Some settled where water was freely available, eventually developing agriculture, but others moved on as nomadic hunters and gatherers, searching for pasture and sufficient water to permit Man and animals to survive.

The early inhabitants of the UAE may have been hunter-gatherers who ventured into desert Arabia from the Fertile Crescent, living partly by exploiting natural food resources, on land and in the shallow inshore waters of the Gulf, and partly from the flocks of sheep and goats that they brought with them.

Over the centuries, the lifestyle changed. By around 5,000 years ago, agriculture had reached the Al Ain area, while at about the same time, the people learned how to exploit the reserves of copper ore in the mountains, developing a valuable export trade with Mesopotamia and the Indus Valley. Pearls harvested from the Gulf may also have been among the commodities traded, for pearls have been found on some of the oldest sites in the Emirates.

The people of the Emirates have always been involved in maritime commerce, the country's strategic location allowing them to act as middlemen between East and West.

By 2000 years ago, around the beginning of the Christian era, the trading network reached Rome in the West and to China in the East, as well as down the coast of East Africa and across land into Central Asia.

In the early 7th Century AD, the religion of Islam was revealed to the Prophet Mohammed (PBUH), and the inhabitants of the UAE were swift to adopt the new faith. As the Islamic State grew, so the trading connections were consolidated, and by the 14th Century AD, the sailors of the United Arab Emirates were amongst the most skilled anywhere in the Indian Ocean.

Historians and archaeologists have yet to determine when the island of Abu Dhabi was first occupied, although pottery dating to the first few centuries of the Christian era has been found on the island. The current settlement, however, appears to have been founded in the middle of the 18th Century AD.

According to tribal legend, a hunting party from the Liwa Oasis were following the tracks of a gazelle near the coast and came to a shallow inlet of the sea, which the gazelle had crossed to a nearby island. Following its tracks onto the island, the hunters found that they led to a spring. Recognising the importance of finding fresh water on the island, the hunters went back to Liwa, and reported to their leader, Sheikh Dhiyab bin Isa, who instructed that a settlement was to be established on the island, which he called Abu Dhabi, Father of, or Possession of the gazelle. That settlement, founded in around 1761, has now become today's city of Abu Dhabi.

In 1795, Sheikh Dhiyab's son, Sheikh Shakhbut, decided to move his headquarters from Liwa to Abu Dhabi Island, and built a fort to protect the valuable source of fresh water. Much expanded over the years, the fort, now known as the Qasr Al Hisn or Old Fort, still stands on the same location, though today it is surrounded not by a few scattered palm trees but by a modern metropolis.

During the course of the 18th and early 19th Centuries, two major tribal alliances existed in the area which now comprises the UAE. In the Northern Emirates, the Al Qawasim, who still rule Sharjah and Ras al-Khaimah, were the dominant power, also controlling much of the southern Iranian coast and also the islands of Greater and Lesser Tunb and Abu Musa, near the mouth of the Gulf.

To the west, the Bani Yas, with their centre on Abu Dhabi island, forged alliances with the Manasir of Liwa, the nomadic Awamir and the Dhawahir, also controlled the offshore islands, many of which were used as bases for the pearling industry.

In January 1820, the Sheikhs of the area signed agreements with the British and later agreed to observe a truce at sea during the pearling season. This truce was at first renewed annually but became permanent in 1854, leading to the emergence of the name The Trucial States, which survived until the formation of the UAE in 1971.

From 1855 to 1909, Abu Dhabi was ruled by Sheikh Zayed bin Khalifa, or Zayed the Great, as he was known. Grandson of Sheikh Shakhbut bin Dhiyab, he was also the grandfather of President His Highness Sheikh Zayed. During his lengthy reign, Abu Dhabi grew to become the dominant power in southeastern Arabia.

Much of his power derived from Abu Dhabi's control of the pearling trade in the southern Gulf, which provided a substantial economic return. By 1900, there were

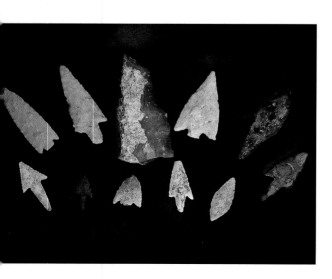

scarcely enough men to work on the **1200** boats involved in the business. The First World War, however, dealt a heavy blow to the trade, as did the world economic depression of the late **1920s** and early **1930s**. The invention of the cultured pearl by Japan finally ruined the trade, which had lasted for around **5,000** years. Abu Dhabi fell on hard times.

There was, however, a new source of revenue on the horizon. Oil had already been found elsewhere in the Gulf and in January **1939**, Sheikh Shakhbut bin Sultan of Abu Dhabi signed an exploration concession with an international oil consortium, the Iraq Petroleum Company, which included the forerunners of today's BP, Shell and Exxon-Mobil. Exploration commenced after the Second World War, with the first well being drilled at Ras Sadr, north east of Abu Dhabi, in **1950**. It was nearly another decade before commercial deposits of oil were found. Oil was first exported in **1962** from the offshore Umm Shaif field, to be followed by the onshore Bab field the next year.

During the **1950s**, political change had begun to make its way to the Gulf region. In **1947**, Britain had granted independence to India and Pakistan, and the routes through the Gulf were no longer as important. Through its Political Resident in the region, based in Bahrain, the British government began to encourage the Trucial States to work with each other. The Trucial Oman Levies, a British-officered force that was the origin of the UAE Armed Forces, was founded in **1951** to help improve security in the desert areas and became the Trucial Oman Scouts in **1953**. The next year, the Trucial States Council, comprising the Rulers of the seven emirates, was founded, providing a regular opportunity for them to get together, something that had not happened for nearly **50** years. The Council, with British support, also began a small-scale development programme.

In **1966**, Sheikh Shakhbut, who had ruled Abu Dhabi since **1928**, abdicated in favour of his younger brother, H.H. Sheikh Zayed. Eager to improve the lot of his people, H.H. Sheikh Zayed promptly began putting the oil revenues to work, also extending grants to the Northern Emirates, which lacked the same source of income.

This spirit of collaboration was to prove its value in early **1968** when the British announced that they would be withdrawing from the Gulf by the end of **1971** as part of a programme of withdrawing all of their military forces from East of Suez. Recognising the need to bring the Emirates closer together to face the challenge of political change, H.H. Sheikh Zayed met with the Ruler of Dubai, the late H.H. Sheikh Rashid bin Saeed Al Maktoum and the two agreed to form a federation, which they invited the other states to join. To encourage his colleagues, H.H. Sheikh Zayed announced that the oil revenues of Abu Dhabi were henceforth to be "at the service of all the Emirates".

A Federation of Arab Emirates, including Sharjah, Ras al-Khaimah, Fujairah, Ajman and Umm al Quwain, as well as Qatar and Bahrain, was promptly established and work began on the creation of a new federal structure which would bring strength in unity, while permitting each participating Emirate to maintain a large measure of its own sovereignty.

As the date for the departure of the British drew closer, however, Qatar and Bahrain decided to opt for the status of separate states. In July **1971**, the Rulers of the seven Trucial States met in Dubai and an agreement was reached on the formation of the United Arab Emirates. Six chose to join at the outset, with the seventh, Ras al-Khaimah, finally joining early in **1972**.

H.H. Sheikh Zayed was elected President by his fellow Rulers, with H.H. Sheikh Rashid of Dubai as Vice President. On 1st December 1971, the old agreements with the British were formally terminated and on 2nd December, the flag of the new state was raised for the first time, marking the birth of the UAE.

In the thirty years that have followed, H.H. Sheikh Zayed has led his country through a process of development that is remarkable. Drawing on a vision that first evolved while he was his brother's representative in Al Ain in the 1950s and keeping to his promise to utilise Abu Dhabi's oil revenues in the service of the people, he has earned, justly, the title of "Father of the Nation". In so doing, he has, been helped by his own experience of two eras, from the poverty of the period between the two World Wars and then before the coming of oil to the ever-growing wealth that has flowed since the first barrel of oil was exported nearly forty years ago.

Statistics on schools, hospitals, roads, housing and other services provide some of the evidence of the progress that has been made. Among the most remarkable achievements, however, has been the way in which this once desert country has become an oasis of green. While much of the land is still desert, over 140 million trees have been planted in a programme of afforestation driven by H.H. Sheikh Zayed's own determination to roll back the sands. In the city of Abu Dhabi, some two dozen parks and nearly 1,500 hectares (3,700 acres) of grass are watered by electronically controlled sprinkler systems and are decorated by spectacular fountains, providing ample green spaces in which the inhabitants of the UAE's modern capital can relax.

Inland, the road to H.H. Sheikh Zayed's beloved city of Al Ain, around 160 km, (100 miles) east of Abu Dhabi, is a six-lane highway divided by a constantly watered central reservation planted with palm trees, bougainvilleas, oleanders and other flowering plants, while a thick belt of trees on either side keeps the desert at bay. When H.H. Sheikh Zayed was a boy, the route was nothing more than camel tracks stretching through the sand dunes.

Today, the proven hydrocarbon reserves of the United Arab Emirates are 98 billion barrels of oil, 10 per cent of the world's total and the third largest after those of Saudi Arabia and Iraq and 6.13 trillion cubic metres of gas, 4 per cent of the world's total and fourth largest after those of Russia, Iran and Qatar. Production at current rates can continue for well over a hundred years, providing a guarantee of future prosperity for the country's population, now just over 3 million. Of the oil reserves, 92 billion barrels are in the Emirate of Abu Dhabi, which remains the major producer both of oil and of Government revenues.

The change that has been made possible by the oil revenues has been achieved at remarkable speed. For those who recall the poor coastal settlement of Abu Dhabi in the 1950s, it must seem almost unbelievable. In the pages that follow, aspects of that change are illustrated. The credit for it lies with H.H. Sheikh Zayed, a Father of the Nation, indeed.

It is worth recalling, though, that the wealth of Abu Dhabi has not benefited only the UAE. H.H. Sheikh Zayed is well known for his belief that it is important that his people learn about their heritage and history. It is, therefore, particularly appropriate that he has funded the building of a new dam at Marib in Yemen, permitting agriculture to flourish once again in the land his ancestors left so many centuries ago.

Chapter 1
The History of The Emirate of Abu Dhabi

THE TOMBS AND STONE BUILDINGS OF SITES AT UMM AN NAR AND HILLI IN Al Ain suggest that the people of ancient times faced a different, wetter climate than that of today. It would appear that those early civilizations lived in a land of great fertility. First excavated by Danish archaeologists in the 50s and 60s, these sites indicate that a flourishing community dwelt there in prehistoric times, before some natural phenomena brought about a drastic climatic change. In the picture above, a cat, the favourite pet of the Prophet Mohammed PBUH, strolls by the reconstructed burial mound in Hilli Garden giving scale to this impressive tomb. Above the triangular window is a carving chiselled on the rock showing two oryx with long horns and two human forms. The carving depicts life in the Al Ain area five thousand years ago when the plains at the foot of Jebel Hafeet and the Hajar Mountains would have been lush savannah.

THE BANI YAS TRIBE ORIGINATED IN THE MARIB area of Yemen but was forced to migrate when the Marib Dam burst for the final time. Most of the tribe settled in the Liwa area. In 1761, a fresh water spring was discovered by hunters following gazelles on the island now known as Abu Dhabi. This resulted in the Al Bu Falah members of the tribe moving there on a seasonal basis. The male members of the tribe spent their summers fishing and pearling off Abu Dhabi Island and their winters tending to their palms in Liwa. In the 1800s, under the leadership of Sheikh Shakhbut bin Dhiyab, the Al Bu Falah collectively moved to Abu Dhabi Island permanently. They left a wali, a governor or tax collector, to monitor their interests in Liwa, another on Dalma Island and another in the Al Ain Oasis. During the following century the Al Bu Falah prospered from their control of the region's only resources; dates, fish and pearls. Al Hisn Fort, pictured left and above, was built to protect the only fresh water spring on the island.

THE OLD FORT, THE PALACE OF THE RULING Sheikh and therefore the centre of Government and Justice, was once one of the few permanent buildings on Abu Dhabi island. Now renovated and extended beyond its original size, it houses the Centre of Documentation and Research. Although completely surrounded by a rapidly expanding cosmopolitan city, it still represents a large part of the heritage and culture of the people of Abu Dhabi. Numerous exhibitions and educational activities take place within The Cultural Foundation and Al Hisn Fort making it a central point in the lives of people of many different nationalities that live in Abu Dhabi.

The inset photograph above shows Al Hisn Fort and camels. Camels were once the only means of transport on the island. It was not until 1947 that the first motor vehicle arrived on the island via cargo ship. Abu Dhabi had an even longer wait for tarmacadam roads. Merchants, traders, divers and fishermen built barasti homes, made of palm tree fronds and lived within easy reach of the shores.

The lower photograph shows how the city's road grid was set out once tarmac roads were laid and the city began to take shape. Even at this stage Al Hisn Fort was isolated from the rest of the city by the developing road system.

IN 1954, THE LATE RONALD CODRAI TOOK THE aerial view of Al Hisn Fort and the Residence of the British Resident Political Officer. The photograph shows the proximity of the Residence to the Fort and the sparse housing and vegetation on the island at that time. Both the Fort and the Residence stood in isolated splendour away from what little settlement there was at that time.

The modern aerial photograph shows how the city has developed around the Fort and Residence. The inset photograph shows H.H. Sheikh Zayed bin Sultan Al Nahyan and his brother H.H. Sheikh Shakbut bin Sultan Al Nahyan outside Al Hisn Fort. It is interesting to note that the Khunjar was still worn as a traditional part of the national dress at that time.

THE NEED FOR PEACEFUL INTERVENTION between the disputed areas in the region known as Trucial Oman, lead to the formation of the Trucial Oman Levies (TOL) in 1951. The region called Trucial Oman stretched across the entire peninsula. The TOL became the Trucial Oman Scouts (TOS) which was founded in 1953. Al Jahili Fort, which stands near the birthplace of H.H. Sheikh Zayed, was the headquarters of the TOS. The TOS formed a mobile policing force throughout the present day Emirates and adjoining Oman and served as a mediating team which settled many land and water disputes. The TOS became the fledgling United Defence Force of the newly declared United Arab Emirates on the 2nd December 1971.

THE INSET PHOTOGRAPHS SHOW THE redevelopment of the coastline which occurred as areas were reclaimed from the sea and roads were built. The once sleepy fishing and pearling village is rapidly changing into a city of the 21st century. Building a modern city from almost nothing took patience and time but with H.H. Sheikh Zayed's foresight and determination the seemingly impossible happened. For centuries, the local population lived a simple life with barasti huts for shelter and fishing, pearling and trading as their only source of income. They have had little time to adjust to this enormous leap forward. With courage and wisdom, H.H. Sheikh Zayed led his people from the 18th to the 21st century, he has enabled them to live in a cosmopolitan business society whilst retaining their Islamic culture and values.

Following page: The satellite photograph shows The Emirate of Abu Dhabi stretching towards Jebel Hafeet on the border with Oman to the east and southwards to the Empty Quarter.

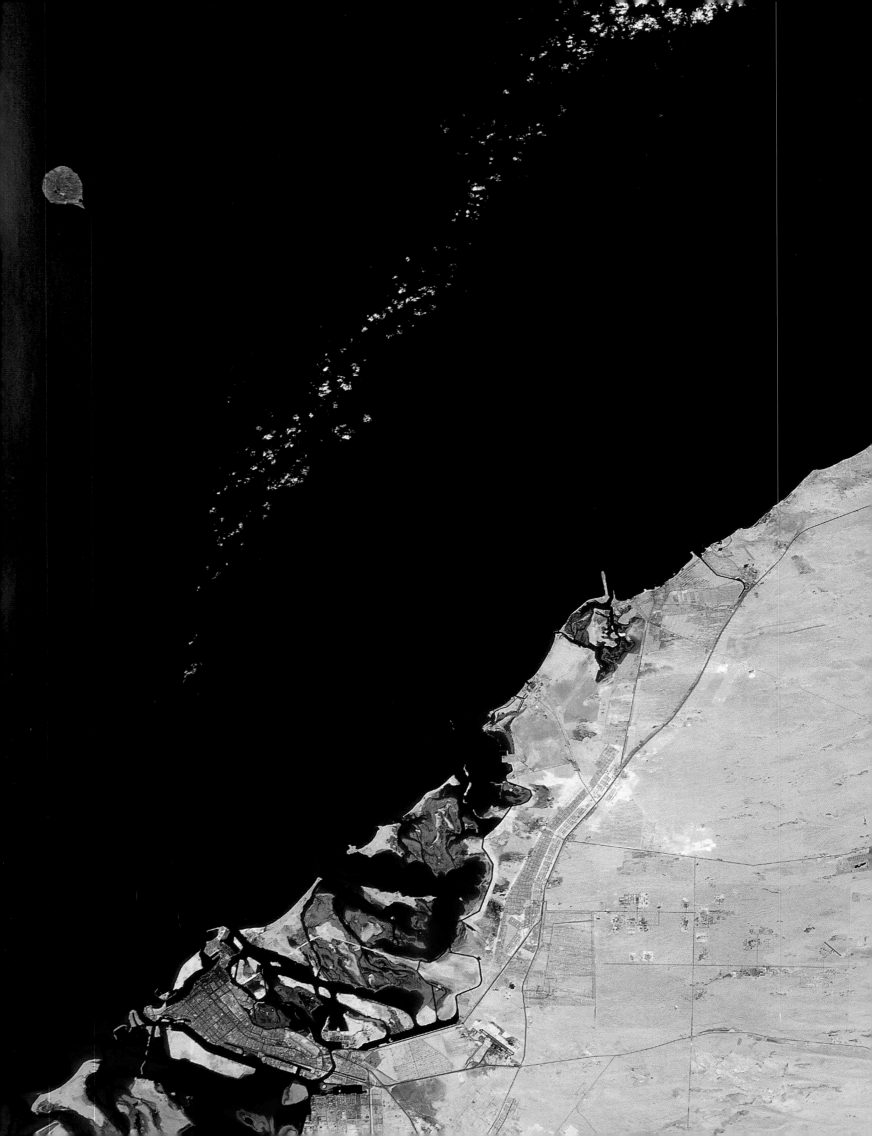

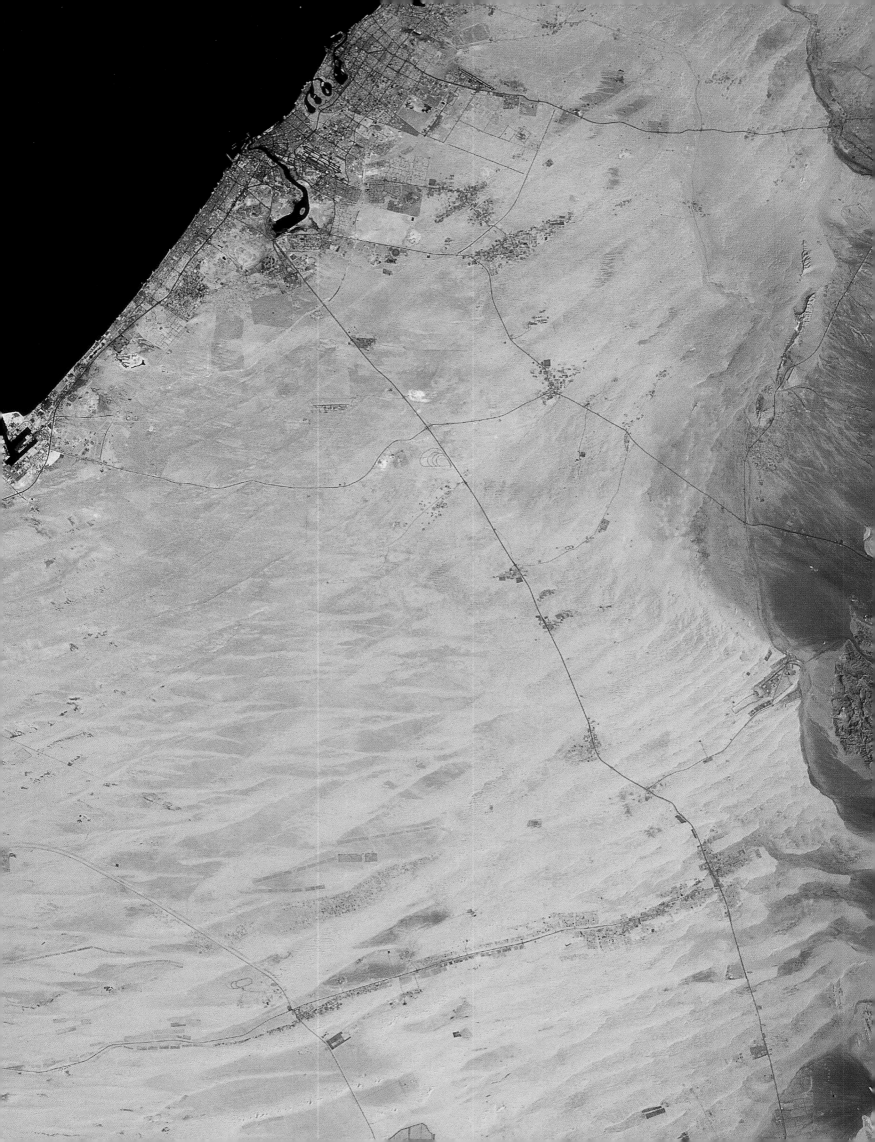

Chapter 2
A Seafaring Nation

THE PEARLING INDUSTRY ON THE GULF COAST OF THE UAE HAS A LONG recorded history. It will never be known when the people of the Emirates first began to harvest the pearls of the Gulf. Individual pearls have been found on archaeological sites that date back to the late Stone Age, six or seven thousand years ago. Archaeologists believe that the 'fish eyes' from the Gulf referred to in ancient Babylonian cuneiform texts may well have been pearls. Al-Idrisi mentions that in 1154 Julfar was already a major pearling centre. The Portuguese writer Duarte Barbosa recorded in 1517 that: 'Here (Julfar) is a very great fishery as well, as of large pearls; and the Moors of Honnuz come hither to buy them and carry them to India and many other lands.' The Portuguese traveller Pedro Teixeira mentions that a fleet of 50 terradas sailed from Julfar every year to the pearl beds. It was the growing European interest in Gulf pearls that led to the tour by the Venetian state jeweller, Gasparo Balbi, in 1580.

The people of Abu Dhabi relied on pearling as a major, if seasonal, form of employment and it formed an important part of the national economy.

Indeed, the name The Trucial States, by which the UAE was formerly known, was derived from a series of maritime truces agreed during the nineteenth century by the various rulers. These truces were introduced with British help and were designed to maintain peace at sea during the pearling season. Many of those engaged in the industry would return home inland between seasons; others travelled abroad in search of fresh oyster beds. British historical records from the late nineteenth century refer to divers from the area travelling to Sri Lanka to work on the pearl beds there once the season in the Gulf was over.

THE SEAS OF THE ARABIAN GULF HAVE MARINE life in abundance and for centuries the people of Abu Dhabi have been skilled seafarers and fishermen. Seafaring is part of the heritage of these people and has sustained them throughout history when other natural resources were scarce. The region's only natural resources were dates, pearls and fish. During the winter months

most of the able-bodied men were employed at sea with the pearling fleet. During the summer, the men, women and children left for the cooler, shadier oases of Liwa and AI Ain. Since nearly all of the inhabitants of Abu Dhabi Island were involved with the sea in some way, homes and businesses naturally evolved around the seashores.

THE WATERS AROUND THE ISLANDS JUST OFF Abu Dhabi offered the best pearling beds. As the demand for pearls grew so did the numbers involved with the industry, both at sea and on land. At the peak of the pearling trade in the 1900s, a flotilla of some twelve hundred boats, four hundred from Abu Dhabi alone, was home to thousands of sailors for up to five months at a time. The spectacle of the flotilla racing for home at the end of the gruelling pearling season can now be imagined with modern aerial photography of a traditional dhow race. Sailing is part of Abu Dhabi's culture; the people's love of the sea and the pleasure they get from it is reflected in the numerous sailing and rowing races that take place throughout the year.

ALONGSIDE THE TRADITIONAL METHODS of shipbuilding, new techniques have been introduced to the industry. Dhow building is a time-honoured craft amongst the Arabian people. The traditional skills and painstaking care put into the wooden dhows that are typical of the region has been passed down to today's generation who practice in the boat-building yards of Bateen. With Abu Dhabi's seafaring history, the people had to have the skill and knowledge to build boats that would serve them well in their maritime endeavours.

A MODERN PATROL BOAT OF THE UAE Navy patrols the lower Gulf against the distant backdrop of the tower blocks of the Abu Dhabi skyline. The continuing expansion of Abu Dhabi Ship Building Company has enabled them to gain substantial contracts from the UAE Armed Forces to upgrade a series of six patrol boats. While ADSB will have complete responsibility

for the complex upgrades to be undertaken at its facilities in Mussafa, it will team up with other international firms who will serve as subcontractors in the completion of the project. The major expansion of the ADSB shipyard will increase its capacity for military and commercial shipbuilding and repair services by around 400% over the present level.

THE ABU DHABI SHORELINE WAS GRACED BY simple one-storey buildings and small fishing boats which were pulled ashore after the day's work was done. Today the shore is edged with the beautifully tended Corniche fronting the dramatic towering buildings that are now the homes and work places for the residents of Abu Dhabi. A stately racing dhow sails taut in a northwesterly wind against the backdrop of Abu Dhabi's modern skyline.

Chapter 3
The Arrival of Aviation

IN 1929, THE FIRST FLYING boats of the British Royal Air Force flew out from England and were based at Basra on the river Euphrates. Six aircraft of 203 Squadron conducted reconnaissance flights all over the Middle East and India. The purpose of these flights was to find suitable landing places, both on sea and land, for refuelling and passenger transfer. These landing areas would be used by both flying boats and fixed-wing aircraft for carrying mail from England to the far flung outposts of the British Empire, including India, Singapore, Hong Kong, Australia and New Zealand. The pilots of 203 Squadron visited all the ruling Sheikhs on the Trucial Coast during their search for suitable landing places. The first aircraft to land of Abu Dhabi alighted on 19th May 1930; the pilots met with Sheikh Shakbut bin Sultan in AI Hisn Fort on Abu Dhabi Island and were granted permission to reconnoitre the area. A suitable landing area was found near the present day naval base. When the aircraft was ready to depart, Sheikh Shakbut and his party accompanied the pilots for a conducted tour of the aircraft. At the time aircraft were constructed of wood and canvas, a fact that became obvious when a member of the Sheikh's party put his foot through the wing. The squadron F540 operational record tells us that swift repairs were made and the aircraft departed safely.

AFTER THE SECOND WORLD WAR A VARIETY OF AIRCRAFT used the old graded landing ground in Abu Dhabi. The first aircraft of Gulf Air, an Avro Anson, commenced scheduled flights in 1947. The Avro Anson, with a capacity of seven passengers, was replaced by the De Havilland Dove and later the four engine De Havilland Heron. In addition, many military aircraft used the landing ground as they went about their business of supporting the British Empire. The main picture shows a Blackburn Beverly of 34 Squadron. BP supplied the fuel for the amazing variety of aircraft that passed through Abu

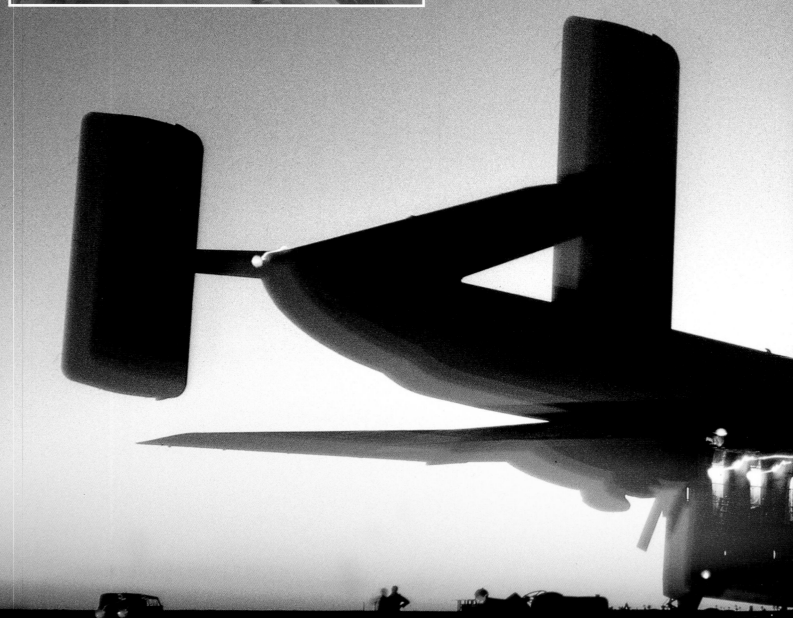

Dhabi. The fuel, contained in 45-gallon drums, was carried by cargo ship from BP's refinery in Basra to an area approximately four miles off shore of Abu Dhabi. The drums were then taken by lighter to the shore were they were floated and finally rolled to the landing ground. All the resident military party would be required to help with the landing of each cargo of 100 drums. One Beverly aircraft would require about 50 drums of fuel on its outward journey and another 50 on its return. Fuel supplies had to be constantly replenished from the BP's refinery in Iraq.

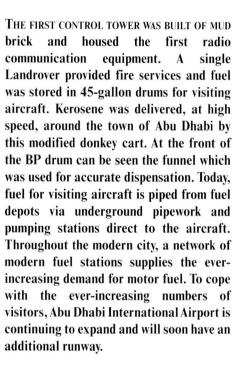

THE FIRST CONTROL TOWER WAS BUILT OF MUD brick and housed the first radio communication equipment. A single Landrover provided fire services and fuel was stored in 45-gallon drums for visiting aircraft. Kerosene was delivered, at high speed, around the town of Abu Dhabi by this modified donkey cart. At the front of the BP drum can be seen the funnel which was used for accurate dispensation. Today, fuel for visiting aircraft is piped from fuel depots via underground pipework and pumping stations direct to the aircraft. Throughout the modern city, a network of modern fuel stations supplies the ever-increasing demand for motor fuel. To cope with the ever-increasing numbers of visitors, Abu Dhabi International Airport is continuing to expand and will soon have an additional runway.

FOUR HAWKER HUNTERS OF THE FLEDGLING
Abu Dhabi Defence Force fly in immaculate
formation over the junction of Airport
Road and the Corniche. The lead aircraft
was flown by Maj. Graham Hounsel, the
Squadron Commander flanked by Maj.
John Stewart-Smith and Jim Brown with
Capt. Jim Parker in the box. The photo-
graph was taken in 1971 by Capt. Dan
Carter from the only Hunter FR10 in the
Abu Dhabi Defence Force. The original
International Airport was constructed on
an open plain at Bateen adjacent to the old
Maqta crossing which had once been the
only access from the mainland to Abu Dhabi
island. The area surrounding the runway
was extensive tidal salt flat which can be
clearly seen on the inset photograph.
Subsequently, the area was dredged and
reclamation work transformed the shape of
Abu Dhabi Island. As the oil business
boomed, it soon became clear that a larger
airport was needed. A new international
airport was opened and Bateen became a
military airport that is also used by Abu
Dhabi Aviation for supporting the oil fields.
In turn, the growing requirement for housing and urban development will lead to the
closure of Bateen airport. All air traffic
will soon use the new International Airport
or the airport in Al Ain. A Civic Centre will
be built across the old Bateen runway.

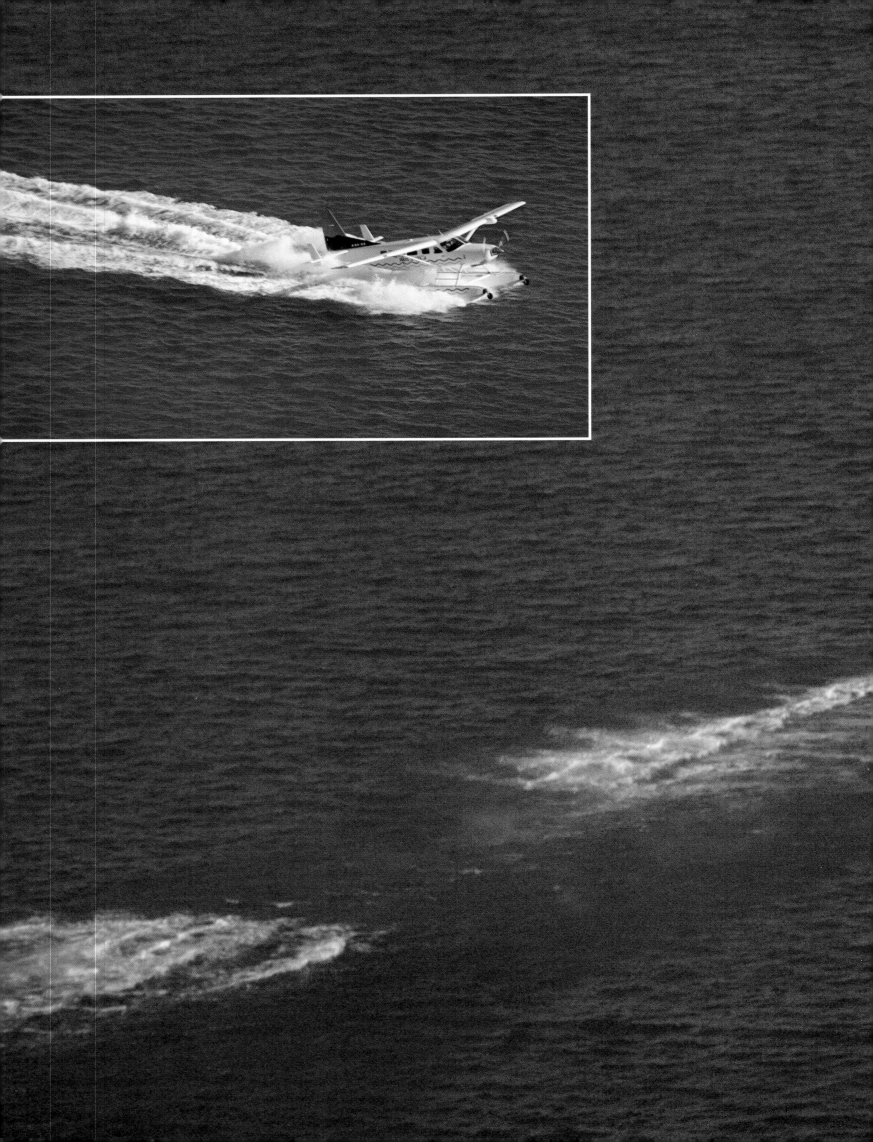

THE FIRST USE OF FLYING BOATS BY THE BRITISH ROYAL AIR FORCE IN THE MIDDLE EAST WAS TO reconnoitre for landing areas across the region to provide a reliable route for the transport of airmail to the far-flung corners of the Empire. The Singapore flying boats of No.203 Squadron, based in Basra, Iraq, carried the various political agents to meet the Rulers and Sheikhs throughout this area. The RAF aircrews often flew the local rulers, including H.H. Sheikh Shakhbut Bin Sultan Al Nahyan, then Ruler of Abu Dhabi, out to their pearling fleets in the Arabian Gulf. Such proving flights led to the implementation of the British Empire Postal Service and all communities at the various landing points benefited dramatically from this new, cheap and revolutionary speedy method of communication. At once, the small and isolated settlements around the Gulf were able to communicate with the outside world. Today, both business people and tourists alike enjoy the dramatic water take off and landing of the Cessna Caravan floatplanes which carry them on the 29 minute flight from Abu Dhabi to Dubai on the new "Emirates Link". The versatile Caravan is used in a variety of roles in every country of the world. DHL alone has a fleet of over 250 such aircraft which operate around the clock to feed express air packages to their larger aircraft for international distribution. Urgent small packages from Dubai to Abu Dhabi are carried within the floats of this amphibious aircraft.

THE BEGINNINGS OF AVIATION IN ABU DHABI WERE modest. A landing strip with a small control tower and terminal were first built in what is now downtown Abu Dhabi, on the site of the present television and radio complex. With part of the income from oil, in 1967 a completely new International Airport, with a runway length of 3,200m was built 15 km from the growing city, near the Maqta crossing, at the inner end of the island. In 1970, a new large passenger terminal and many auxiliary buildings were opened to cope with the increasing flow of passengers and cargo. Today, this airport is used only as a centre for military and private aviation, and will soon be developed as a park and civic centre. In 1982, a new International Airport was opened on the mainland, a few kms. from the island, to handle the growing traffic. This airport is now too small. An extra terminal is being added and a new, second runway will be built.

SABKHA IS THE ARABIC TERM FOR SALTY, MARSHY GROUND, OFTEN CLOSE TO THE COAST. DURING THE winter season, occasional rains fall and saturate the ground presenting a dangerous surface for both animals and vehicles. During the intensive heat of the summer months the *sabkha* dries out and cracks making a dramatic white landscape of glistening salt residue. The new Abu Dhabi International Airport was built on elevated ground above the adjacent *sabkha* in the early 1980s. The rapid development of international air traffic has led to the plans for the construction of a second runway and an additional passenger terminal. GAMCO, the Gulf Aircraft Maintenance Company, a joint venture between the Government of Abu Dhabi and the regional carrier, Gulf Air, in which the Government also has a share, occupies the largest part of the airport. Its extensive facilities provide for the servicing and maintenance of many international airlines. The high quality of their service can be realised from their recent winning of a contract to refurbish a number of flying tankers of the British Royal Air Force, shown here in a dramatic night time rollout. The extensive facilities and capabilities of GAMCO include a huge hangar where all the aircraft of Emirates Airline received their new logos. The inset picture shows H.E. Sheikh Hamdan bin Mubarak Al Nahyan, the Chairman of the Abu Dhabi Department of Civil Aviation, receiving a trophy on the occasion for the opening of the new hanger.

Chapter 4
The Discovery of Oil

ABU DHABI RECEIVED ITS FIRST REVENUES from oil exploration following the signature on 11th January 1939 on a concession agreement with a British-led consortium of oil companies, including British Petroleum, Shell, the French firm TOTAL, Exxon and Mobil and Partex. The consortium, known as the Iraq Petroleum Company, IPC, operated in the Emirates as Petroleum Development (Trucial Coast), which changed its name to the Abu Dhabi petroleum Company, ADPC, after the discovery of commercial deposits of oil in the Emirate.

In the 1930s, oil deposits discovered in Bahrain and Saudi Arabia had suddenly focused the attention of the international oil companies on the region. Following a number of preliminary survey expeditions, agreements were signed by IPC with all of the Rulers of the Trucial Coast.

BRITISH PETROLEUM, ONCE KNOWN AS THE Anglo-Persian Oil Company, after the country where it began, and the dominant partner in IPC, first sent a young geologist to Abu Dhabi in 1934 at the invitation of Sheikh Shakhbut who sought help in the discovery of more water wells. Desert surveys by the IPC geological team, accompanied on some of their journeys by H.H. Sheikh Zayed bin Sultan Al Nahyan, then less than twenty, encouraged the company to proceed with the signing of a concession agreement.

The 1939 agreement with Sheikh Shakhbut of Abu Dhabi gave the company exclusive rights to the oil that was believed to lie under the territory of Abu Dhabi. The outbreak of World War II put a halt to further exploration, however, and it was not until the mid 1940s, after the war had come to an end, that the first detailed exploration got under way in Abu Dhabi. A first well at Ras Sadr, north-east of Abu Dhabi city, was drilled in 1950, and was at the time the deepest well ever

drilled in the Middle East, reaching a depth of just over 13,000 feet. It proved, however, to be a "dry hole," and it was not until the late 1950s that drilling at Murban, in the desert, proved the commercial viability of what became known as the Bab field, which, still producing four decades later, is the foundation of the country's prosperity.

The inset photograph shows the first BP petrol station in Abu Dhabi, which was soon followed by a network of stations throughout the Emirate. The intensive development of the oil industry demanded faster and more reliable method of delivering oil field equipment from the United States, Europe and around the globe, a vacuum that was filled by the global network of DHL. To this day, just-in-time, routine spare parts and AOG (Aircraft On Ground) spares are delivered via the most sophisticated system the world has ever seen. DHL is investing a further Dhs 5.5 million to expand its operations in the Abu Dhabi Emirate.

In 1953, THE D'ARCY EXPLORATION
Company, a British Petroleum subsidiary,
was awarded the offshore concession in
Abu Dhabi, with BP later establishing Abu
Dhabi Marine Areas (ADMA) to operate
the concession. Systematic exploration of
the seabed began and Das Island, the haunt
of nesting terns and turtles, became the
supply point for the marine operations. A
first survey of the seabed was carried out
with the help of the underwater explorer
Jacques Cousteau, and a promising
location was identified at an area known to
local fishermen as Umm Shaif. In 1958, the
first well was drilled on the structure,
discovering what was to become a giant oil
field. A submarine pipeline was
constructed to connect the Umm Shaif
field with Das Island and in 1962 the first
load of Umm Shaif crude oil was
dispatched from Das to BP's Aden refinery.
An even larger offshore oil field was
discovered at Zakum in 1964 and in recent
years some smaller ones have been
developed or redeveloped in the continuing
search for new deposits.

FOR MORE THAN **20** YEARS DUCAB HAS SUPPLIED MOST OF THE ELECTRIC cables needed to power the development and infrastructure of the Emirate of Abu Dhabi.

Ducab, the UAE's cable company, is owned by the Governments of Abu Dhabi and Dubai, and has built an enviable reputation for quality and customer service. Ducab is proud of the role it has played in "*Powering the UAE Nation*".

Left: Ducab 11kV Powerplus medium voltage cables being laid near the Abu Dhabi breakwater.

Ducab is concerned about safety and reliability and is committed to raising standards. Cables rarely fail, and a large proportion of faults arise due to poor jointing procedures.

Ducab, in close co-operation with the Abu Dhabi electrical utilities, has set up a Jointer Training Academy to help raise skill levels and improve the operational efficiency of the electricity supply network.

Above: Delivery of Ducab Powerplus 33kV Medium Voltage cables on the Abu Dhabi Corniche.
Right: Ducabs' Jointing Academy–setting new training standards.

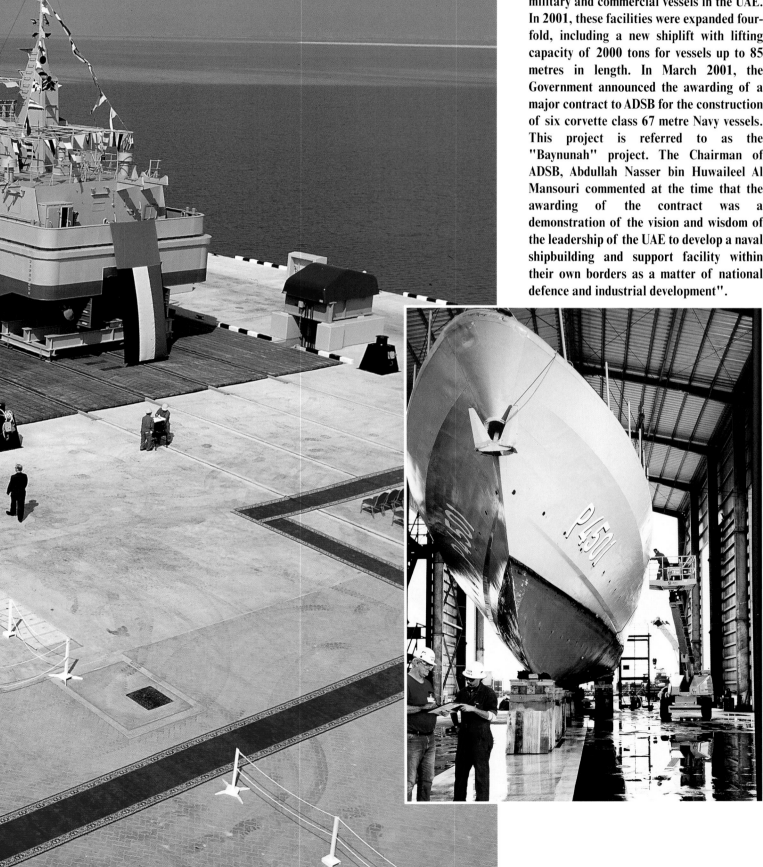

IN **1996**, ABU DHABI SHIP BUILDING COMPANY, established under the framework of the UAE's ambitious military Offsets Programme, began providing state-of-the-art technical and physical capabilities to construct, overhaul and repair complex military and commercial vessels in the UAE. In 2001, these facilities were expanded four-fold, including a new shiplift with lifting capacity of 2000 tons for vessels up to 85 metres in length. In March 2001, the Government announced the awarding of a major contract to ADSB for the construction of six corvette class 67 metre Navy vessels. This project is referred to as the "Baynunah" project. The Chairman of ADSB, Abdullah Nasser bin Huwaileel Al Mansouri commented at the time that the awarding of the contract was a demonstration of the vision and wisdom of the leadership of the UAE to develop a naval shipbuilding and support facility within their own borders as a matter of national defence and industrial development".

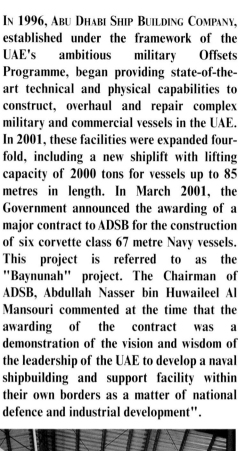

Chapter 5
The Capital — Abu Dhabi

ABU DHABI ISLAND, ON WHICH THE CAPITAL CITY of the Emirate of Abu Dhabi, and of the United Arab Emirates, is located, was once a sparsely populated, seasonal settlement. The elongated, wedge-shaped island was formerly only accessible from the mainland by making a hazardous crossing on foot or by driving cautiously at low tide through the sea. The watchtower built at the crossing is one of the three original buildings remaining on the island and kept residents safe from surprise attack. In the late 1950's a rough causeway was built to ease the crossing and later, in 1969, H.H. Sheikh Zayed inaugurated the 1400-foot, twin-laned Maqta Bridge. In the year 2000, the enormous increase in motor traffic led to an identical bridge being positioned alongside the original one to ease the constant flow of traffic on and off the island.

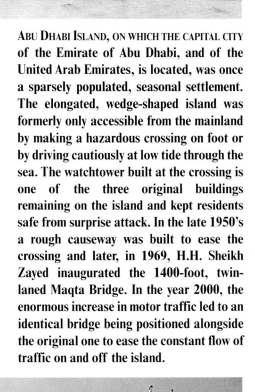

QASR AL HISN, BUILT IN **1795** BY SHEIKH SHAKHBUT BIN Dhiyab, an ancestor of Sheikh Zayed, has changed beyond recognition. Much enlarged from its original size, it is no longer the seat of government or home of the Ruler. Now the Fort is a focal point for the country's heritage, and plans are being drawn up for it to be converted into a museum. Adjacent to the Fort is the Cultural Foundation with a well-stocked public library. The main picture shows the original red & white flag of the Emirate of Abu Dhabi flying over the Fort. The inset pictures show Abu Dhabi as it was in the 1950 & 1960's, a sparsely populated island with people whose lives had changed little over the centuries.

ABU DHABI WAS ONCE A SEASONAL HOME TO FISHERMEN, BOAT builders, pearl divers and pearl merchants who lived and conducted their business within easy access of the seashore. Even when the original homes built of 'arish (palm fronds) and blocks of coral were replaced with more substantial buildings, the absence of vehicles or roads meant that journeys had to be made on foot or by donkey or camel, and, not surprisingly, it was

most convenient for homes and businesses to be within easy access of the seashore. The entrance to the souk (market) was positioned close to the shore so that the goods from the lighters could be carried there easily. The inset photographs show fishing boats anchored or pulled onto the beach after a day at sea. The abundant marine life of the Arabian Gulf has always provided much of the fare of the coastal people.

ABU DHABI'S TRANSFORMATION INTO THE MODERN bustling city it is today started when the oil revenues began to flow in the early 1960s, and was given particular impetus by the accession of HH Sheikh Zayed bin Sultan Al Nahyan as Ruler in August 1966. Determined to ensure that the new-found wealth should be put to good use in the service of the people, he embarked, almost from the day of his accession, on the implementation of plans of which he had long been dreaming. Land was reclaimed along the shoreline to provide the city with the interesting features seen in this aerial shot. This marked the beginning of the Corniche of today. The original grid that was laid out for the city is now almost filled with tarmac and concrete, a stark contrast to the sabkha and sand that is now part of Abu Dhabi's history.

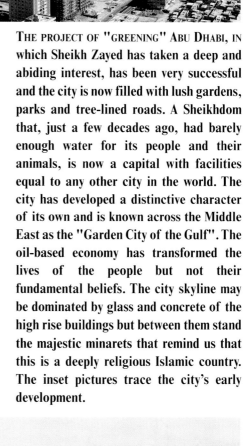

THE PROJECT OF "GREENING" ABU DHABI, IN which Sheikh Zayed has taken a deep and abiding interest, has been very successful and the city is now filled with lush gardens, parks and tree-lined roads. A Sheikhdom that, just a few decades ago, had barely enough water for its people and their animals, is now a capital with facilities equal to any other city in the world. The city has developed a distinctive character of its own and is known across the Middle East as the "Garden City of the Gulf". The oil-based economy has transformed the lives of the people but not their fundamental beliefs. The city skyline may be dominated by glass and concrete of the high rise buildings but between them stand the majestic minarets that remind us that this is a deeply religious Islamic country. The inset pictures trace the city's early development.

Chapter 6
The Garden City – Al Ain

AL AIN, THE SECOND CITY OF THE EMIRATE OF ABU DHABI, LIES 160 KILOMETRES due east of the city of Abu Dhabi. H.H. Sheikh Zayed bin Sultan Al Nahyan was born in Al Ain in 1918 when it was just one of several villages known as the Buraimi Oasis. It was here amongst these oases, surrounded by the hostile desert that H.H. Sheikh Zayed spent his childhood and adolescence. Here he learnt the ways of the Bedu and developed the skills that were to enable him to become the leader he is today. When H.H. Sheikh Zayed became the Governor of Al Ain in 1946 his immediate concern was to stimulate the economy by increasing agricultural output. To do this, more water was needed. He immediately set the men folk to work cleaning and renovating the old falaj system that carried water down from Jebel Hafit. With his own money, he began construction of a new falaj. Al Ain is the Arabic word for spring and today the city is a welcoming oasis for the burgeoning tourist industry.

CAREFULLY PLANNED IRRIGATION, USING THE SUPPLIES OF FRESH WATER which run off the neighbouring Hajar Mountains, enabled Al Ain to develop as a centre for agriculture. Today, lush green fields and palm groves surround Al Ain. Its farms produce much of the fresh fruit and vegetables for the region. Planned development and meticulous maintenance has earned Al Ain the title "The Garden City of the Arabian Gulf". In 2000 the city won 2nd place in the "Nations in Bloom" competition held in Washington DC, quite an achievement since Al Ain was competing against a large number of cities from around the world.

In 1964, a team of Danish archaeologists discovered one of Abu Dhabi's most significant locations during an excavation of the area. The restored Hilli Tomb now stands in the centre of Hilli Garden. It is a circular tomb made of carefully shaped blocks with decorative relief carvings of men and animals on the outside wall and a small triangular entrance above ground. Further excavation in the Hilli area has unearthed a number of graves and a settlement site dating back to prehistoric times, suggesting that a flourishing community lived around the oasis at a time when the climate was milder than it is today.

AL AIN'S HISTORY IS INEVITABLY LINKED WITH those other villages and tribes that inhabited the area once known as the Buraimi Oasis. Three of the villages were subjects of the Ruler of Oman and the others of the Ruler of Abu Dhabi. The position of the villages at the crossroads of the desert trade routes and the availability of fresh water, grazing and shade, made the Buraimi Oasis a very desirable place. Claims and border disputes over land ownership continued for centuries. The majority of disputes were centred around tribal loyalty, either to Oman or Abu Dhabi. Saudi Arabia also made claims to the territory and had an influential presence at various times. The original villages have now disappeared and appear as suburban names in the sprawl of Al Ain. The beautiful tree-lined roads continue around the city via numerous roundabouts depicting the region's Islamic heritage and culture.

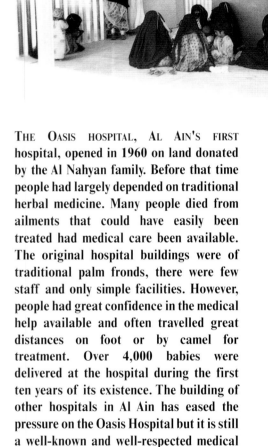

THE OASIS HOSPITAL, AL AIN'S FIRST
hospital, opened in 1960 on land donated
by the Al Nahyan family. Before that time
people had largely depended on traditional
herbal medicine. Many people died from
ailments that could have easily been
treated had medical care been available.
The original hospital buildings were of
traditional palm fronds, there were few
staff and only simple facilities. However,
people had great confidence in the medical
help available and often travelled great
distances on foot or by camel for
treatment. Over 4,000 babies were
delivered at the hospital during the first
ten years of its existence. The building of
other hospitals in Al Ain has eased the
pressure on the Oasis Hospital but it is still
a well-known and well-respected medical
centre.

BEFORE THE OIL REVENUES FLOWED, THE VAST majority of people of Abu Dhabi could not read or write. Those who could read learned to do so by using the Quran, the only book available at the time. At 12 or 13 boys followed their fathers into pearling, fishing, farming or tending animals whilst young girls learnt from their female relatives the traditional skills needed to be a wife and mother. Today opportunities abound for both boys and girls who receive primary, secondary and higher education.

Over the years Al Ain has become an established seat of learning. In 1977 H.H. Sheikh Zayed inaugurated the UAE's first university, with its numerous faculties offering ever expanding opportunities for higher education to the people of the Emirates. In 1994, the first students graduated from the newly accredited Faculty of Medicine and Health Science. During the current academic year it was a statistical fact that there were more female students than male.

WHEN SHEIKH ZAYED WAS APPOINTED WALI OF Al Ain in 1946 he was already a well-known and respected young man. Wise beyond his years, he had assimilated knowledge through experience. With little formal education, his natural inquisitiveness enabled him to learn from everything and everyone around him. He watched, listened and learnt from tribal elders as they discussed the daily struggle to survive in their harsh environment. He roamed the desert and mountains perfecting his skills in the traditional practices of riding, hunting and falconry. As respect for him grew, the elders of the tribes often compared him to his grandfather Sheikh Zayed bin Khalifa, known as Sheikh Zayed the Great. First as Governor of Al Ain, then as Ruler of the Emirate of Abu Dhabi since 1966 and President of the United Arab Emirates since its creation in 1971, Sheikh Zayed's primary concern has always been the needs of the people. With wise and generous use of oil revenues, he has eradicated the poverty and neglect the people had endured for centuries. Now a much-respected leader on the world stage he has remained an approachable, much loved man with a deep commitment to his country and his people.

MODERN VILLAS HAVE NOW REPLACED THE simple *barasti* or mud brick homes that once housed the inhabitants of AI Ain. Water gushes on demand from internal plumbing and only in the most isolated places do people have to carry and store water in the ways they did in olden times. The plans H.H. Sheikh Zayed laid down during his twenty years as governor of AI Ain have now come to fruition.

Located between the austere Hajar mountain range and the harsh desert, Al Ain is now a modern, green and attractive city with well planned, shady roads, immaculate grass, an abundance of flowering plants, public parks and gardens. Tourists and residents alike enjoy the peace and tranquillity that is part of Al Ain's charm whilst finding plenty to amuse and entertain themselves.

Chapter 7
Sports, Leisure & Tourism

WITH THE INFLUX OF EXPATRIATES INTO ABU DHABI IN RECENT years, leisure and sports activities from the West have flourished alongside more traditional pastimes. The climate of Abu Dhabi particularly lends itself to outdoor pursuits that can be practiced during the cooler winter months. Golf is a favourite sport and many people take the opportunity to try their hand at this popular sport. The new Abu Dhabi Golf Course, with its magnificent club house in the shape of a falcon, is just one of several world class greens or browns within the Emirate where golfers can test their skills. Visitors of all ages travel from Japan, the USA and Europe to play this course.

THE TRADITIONAL BEDOUIN LIFE MAY HAVE BEEN harsh but there was always time for relaxation and leisure activities, cementing family and tribal ties and giving rise to the legendary Arabian hospitality. A traveller could expect three days hospitality from his hosts, likewise the host could expect his guest to depart after three days. Whilst the traditional hospitality still exists, the introduction of cars and roads has meant that the three day rule is no longer necessary. Travellers can reach their destination in a matter of hours whereas a few decades ago the journey would have taken days. Tourists and businessmen visit the Rotana Hotels in Abu Dhabi and Al Ain to enjoy their 5 star treatment. Many enjoy the culture and diversity of the Emirate. Abu Dhabi is truly an amazing Emirate and city, named after the gazelle who once roamed free on this island.

THE SEAFARING HISTORY OF THE PEOPLE IS reflected today when local teams compete in the rowing and dhow racing that marks most national holidays. No longer a means of survival in the daily scheme of things, these activities have become a sporting challenge to Abu Dhabi's new generations. The people of the UAE have long depended on the sea for sustenance and are known to consume the largest amount of fish per person in the world. Although some still earn their living by fishing in the Arabian seas, many of Abu Dhabi's residents relax by casting their lines in the abundantly filled ocean. From simple hand-held lines to the complexity of deep sea fishing vessels, fishermen young and old sit, patiently waiting for their catch, spectators to the more vigorous rowing races.

THE ORIGIN OF THE RELATIONSHIP BETWEEN the Arab and his Arabian horse is based on a romantic but practical legend. It is said that a party of men journeyed to visit a wise man, whose name was the Prophet Suleiman. Their original purpose was to talk about religion and having learnt the answers to their questions, they prepared to leave. One of the visitors asked their host for food for their long journey home. In reply, the wise man gave the party an Arabian mare. He told them, "When you need food, put a man on this horse, arm him with a spear, he will hunt like the wind and bring you food". They named the horse "Zad Al Rakeb" meaning "The supplies of the rider" and since that day the Arabs and their horses have depended on each other. The Prophet Suleiman is also remembered by his wise saying "Give a man some food and you'll feed him for a day; Teach a man to hunt and you'll feed him all his life."

CAMELS ARE NATIVE TO THIS PART OF THE world and together with the Oryx, are depicted on prehistoric tombs. Once a beast of burden and an efficient means of transport in the hostile desert environment, the camels and camel handling is an intrinsic part of Arabian culture. Today camels are rarely needed

for transport but used instead for a regional sport. Camel racing is extremely popular with locals and expatriates. Most tourists will see one of these dramatic races during their visit. Racing camels are much prized possessions and often change hands for many thousands of Dirhams.

NOMADIC LIFE WAS ALWAYS INTRINSICALLY tied up with the resources the environment had to offer. This important relationship between the Arab and nature is reflected in modern time by the various agencies commissioned to work on environmental matters in the region. British Petroleum took the lead in the early 1970s and provided intrinsic support for many environmental projects. Pictured above is H.R.H. The Prince of Wales when he visited Al Wathba Lakes where he performed the opening ceremony. Two branches of the Emirates Natural History Group were formed in Abu Dhabi and Al Ain in the 1970s. These amateur organizations laid the foundations of later professional organizations. The Abu Dhabi Island Archeological Survey was

formed in 1995. In turn, ERWDA (the Environmental Research and Wildlife Development Agency) was established in 1996 with the aim of enhancing, developing and protecting the wildlife of the emirate of Abu Dhabi. WWF (the World Wide Fund for Nature) established an office in Abu Dhabi in 2000 to promote their conservation message throughout the region. Her Majesty Queen Elizabeth II is a frequent visitor to the region and is shown above being hosted by His Highness Sheikh Zayed Bin Sultan Al Nayhan in his desert majlis. During this visit the Queen enjoyed seeing the traditional spectacle of falconry. The main central picture shows H.H. Sheikh Zayed entertaining the Commander of the Trucial Oman Scouts in the shade of the walls of Jahili Fort in Al Ain.

TOWERING FOUNTAINS AND BUILDINGS NOW GUSH TO NEW HEIGHTS throughout the Emirate of Abu Dhabi. The fountain shown in the picture at right, below Jebel Hafeet was found using the latest satellite mapping from space. New companies such as NRSC provide this ground breaking technology in association with the Higher Colleges of Technology in their specialised department of CERT, the Centre of Excellence for Applied Research and Training. One of the highest buildings in Abu Dhabi is the Rotana Grand with has a revolving restaurant at its very top which affords splendid views of the entire city by day and night.

Chapter 8
Natural History & Culture

THE NOMADIC ANCESTORS OF THE PEOPLE OF ABU DHABI OWNED VERY little in the way of material goods. A life spent constantly searching for water and pasture necessary for the survival of man and his animals gave little opportunity to gain anything but the most basic possessions. If not wealthy in the material sense, the bedu had a very rich culture based on generosity, hospitality and common-sense justice. The little they had was shared with travellers and there was a strict code of behaviour covering the length of time they would host and protect those they came across on their travels. Without books or the ability to read and write, oral tradition was strong and the only means of preserving their history. While sitting around their desert campfires in the cool evening, tribal history passed from generation to generation in the form of stories, poetry and songs.

LIWA IS THE ANCESTRAL HOME OF THE BANI YAS TRIBE. IT WAS TO THESE villages the tribe migrated after they were forced from Marib in Yemen when the area could no longer support the numbers living there. Liwa is a series of oasis villages scattered over an area interspersed with palm groves which provided shade and dates for the people. Goats and camels were probably their only other means of sustenance. The great distances that separated the people of Liwa from its neighbours could only be crossed on foot or camel back. Since it was not safe to travel alone people usually joined together to journey as part of a camel caravan; a group of travellers were less likely to be troubled on route. Everything needed for the journey had to be carried on the camels since there was little chance of getting further supplies. The only water available was from wells dotted along their route. There was no guarantee that these wells had not dried up.

A DRIVE ALONG THE HIGHWAY FROM THE CAPITAL TO AL AIN IS AN introduction to the beauty and complexity of the sand dunes that line the route. As you shake off the bulldozed tract and leave the orbit of Abu Dhabi's development, the dunes assume a warmer shade of gold, offset by the white of the *sabkha* and the blue-gray gypsum deposits. Nearer Al Ain, a deeper red infuses the sand and the dunes take on hues that range from orange to deep pink. Light and the time of day determine the actual tone, with iron oxides accounting for the redness of the sand. Al Ain has been a crossroads on the desert trade routes for thousands of years with evidence of human settlement dating back at least six or seven thousand years.

WATER, THE ABSOLUTE ESSENTIAL RESOURCE NECESSARY FOR LIFE, HAS been the historical focus of people worldwide. When water becomes available people are drawn to the area and will often settle there, their entire lives revolving around that supply of water. Whilst the men of this region traditionally fought for the right to use the water, it was the women and children who had to fetch and carry the amount needed by each household. Large families and big herds

required an enormous amount of water and the women and children spent many hours drawing water from the closest well. This gave them an opportunity to socialise and pass news between the tribal families. The days were long and hard. The women and older children spent their time fetching water, cooking, searching for wood, raising young children and even tending the animals if the male tribe members were away.

THE ANNIVERSARY OF THE FOUNDING OF THE UNITED ARAB EMIRATES TAKES PLACE EVERY YEAR on the 2nd of December. The first signing of the document which laid down the agreement between the Sheikhs of Abu Dhabi, Dubai, Sharjah, Ajman, Umm Al Quwain, Ras Al Khaimah and Fujeirah took place in Dubai on the 2nd of December 1971. National Day is celebrated throughout the Emirates and here on the Corniche of Abu Dhabi, young ladies in their finest dress dance in the traditional way to the dulcet tunes of the flute and drum. The events take place at the so-called "Volcano" roundabout on the afternoon of the 2nd day of December and continue into the evening. The people of the UAE have seen many dramatic changes since the Federation was formed. These profound changes have provided every citizen with all the facilities and benefits worthy of a country with one of the highest per capita income in the world. It is important for the reader to appreciate that, in the past, it required great skill to survive in the harsh desert environment. It is, therefore, to their great credit that the people of the UAE are determined to maintain their heritage.

THE CHALLENGE OF COMPLETING AN OIL PAINTING OF ANY WORLD RULER CAN BE A DAUNTING prospect even to an accomplished artist. The world famous portrait painter David Shepherd *OBE FRCS GAVA* has been quoted as saying that it is easier to paint a picture of tigers, Arabian Leopards or Oryx than to track and paint a busy Head of State. David had already visited the UAE to complete a painting of Jahili Fort in Al Ain. He returned on a commission to complete a portrait of H.H. Sheikh Zayed and was granted an audience in a garden setting in Al Ain. David realised that this would be his only chance to take the vital reference photographs and he took just one roll of film. On his return to England, he developed the film and to his horror, only one photograph was usable. However he was able to complete his masterful portrait and return to present it to H.H. Sheikh Zayed. The portrait was extremely well received.

Chapter 9
Authors
Acknowledgements

WITH THE HIGHLY SUCCESSFUL LAUNCH OF "NOW & THEN – DUBAI", photographed by my son, Robert, and written by my daughter, Simone, I was propelled, in turn, into the limelight to undertake "Now & Then – Abu Dhabi". Anyone who knows my husband, John, will already know that he is a master of delegation. They will also know that his extensive vocabulary does not include such words as "impossible", "can't be done" or "no way!" With a wave of his arm, he left one day for Oman or Bahrain or Lebanon or UK or the USA leaving me to get on with the research and writing and Nick Crawley, his full time graphic designer to

Of course, we were fortunate that John's military system of doings things was already up and running. His many friends, who had supported him so well in previous books, were all too willing to help us. And help they did, for without them, we would never have reached the printing stage. Our "target-for-tonight" publication date had been set for Spring 2001 and we are pleased that we made it this year at all. Much of the very initial photographic research had already been located but that turned out to be the easy part. We are both very grateful to all the people who helped to transform a jigsaw puzzle into a book.

We would first like to thank His Highness Sheikh Abdullah bin Zayed Al Nahyan, the Federal Minister of Information, His Highness Sheikh Hamdan bin Mubarrak Al Nahyan, Chairman of Abu Dhabi Civil Aviation, who kindly wrote the foreword and His Highness Sheikh Nahyan bin Mubarrak Al Nahyan, the Federal Minister of Education who has always been supportive of our projects; His Highness Sheikh Hamad bin Tahnoon Al Nahyan, Chairman of DUCAB; His Excellency Dr Sheikh Ahmed bin Saif Al Nahyan, Chairman of GAMCO and His Excellency Mohammed bin Habroush Al Suweidi, Chairman of the National Bank of Abu Dhabi. Their staffs were most helpful and we would especially like to thank Dr Peter Hellyer for writing the introduction and picture on page 14 inset, Simon Aspinall and Abdul Salem Amer Lardhi of the UAE Federal Ministry of Information

Special thanks go to David Shepherd *OBE, FRSA, FRGS and GavA* for permission to use his superb oil portrait of His Highness Sheikh Zayed bin Sultan Al Nahyan on page 118. His account of his painting exploits during the days of the Trucial States and later when he came to paint the Arabian Leopard in the days of the UAE was a revelation to hear. We are particularly pleased to be able to support his great lifetime work, the David Shepherd Conservation Foundation. Thanks also to artist Christopher Southcombe, RN for permission to use his wonderful rendition of a pearling dhow on page 30/31.

We met many archivists for the first time, all were unfailingly helpful and though we were not able to use all the pictures which we found, we would like to thank all following archivists: Geoff O'Connor and Peter Kemp & all the staff of the Imperial War Museum (pages 42/43 and inset pages 43, 51); the staff of the Public Records Office at Kew, Paul Dubeck and Matt Jones of Boeing & FP7; Fred Huntley, Terry Daly, Dawn Winn and Adrian Meredith of British Airways; Isha and Mahet of ADCO (back cover); Bill Hunt of The Ministry of Defence photography department; Kim Hearn of the Quadrant Library of Flight International Magazine; Anne Swain of the National Geographic Image Library, Washington; Chris Morton of the Pitts River Museum, Oxford; Gordon Barclay of the British Aerospace Library at Warton (page 14 inset); all at the Public Records Office at Kew; Michael Gassan of the British Petroleum archives, Kevin Dunne of ADCO & BP; Hassan Saigal, Jalal Al Khaled and his predecessor, Nabil Zakhour and finally, Wafa Morda'a all of ADCO; Roger Barcham and especially Andy Whithead of the Abu Dhabi Petroleum Co Ltd. for access to the BP/ADCO/IPC archives (page 40/41, 56/57, 74/75, & page 10, 47, 61, 105, 119, insets) and especial thanks to Antoine Sayegh, GM of the Khahdya Hotel, for (pages 26, 32, 33, 71, 72, 79, 80, 82, 83, 85, 97, 101, 102, 103, 111, 116, 117) for his generous permission to use their extensive library of pictures; finally to all the staff of the photographic archive and the map department of the Royal

Retired members of the Royal Air Force, who were old friends of my husband, were particularly helpful in the making of this book; Sqn. Ldr. John Stewart-Smith, ex-No 1 (Fighter) Sqn. and founder member of the Abu Dhabi Defence Force (pages 24, & 48, 90, inset); John's old friend and supporter, the late Sqn. Ldr Ron Codrai, ex-No 625 Sqn. and No 156 Sqn., Pathfinder Force flying Lancaste (pages 18 and 22 & page 36 inset); Dugold Cameron of No 84 Sqn. for his painting of the Wapiti (page 47 Inset); John Phillips (pages 46/47 & page 24 inset); Bob & Jane McAllen (page 48/49); Jim Hood of No 206 Sqn.; Richard F. Smith of No 203 Sqn; Sqn. Ldr Tony Cunnane of the Red Arrows; Lou Lyddon of the Trucial Oman Scouts (page 24); Ray Deacon of No 37 Sqn; Sqn. Ldr Tom Sheppard, FRGS ARPS, former fighter pilot of No 208 Squadron, author, photographer and ex-Base Commander of RAF Sharjah for his generous help (pages 6/7, 32/33, 44/45, 58/59, 70/71, 72/73, 100/101, & 26, 45, 52, 74, 75, inset); and finally, our thanks to the

many undocumented members of the Royal Air Force who took photographs as part of their duties in the British Empire and Commonwealth so many years ago. Thanks also to Lt Col Moh'd Al Jenaibi of General Headquarters, Abu Dhabi. The photographs by the Royal Air Force are British Crown copyright, and reproduced with the permission of the Controller of Her Britannic Majesty's Stationery Office.

We were pleased to receive the help and contributions of fellow photographers; Dr Gertrude Dyck, known throughout the Emirates as Dr Latifa, for her wonderful early pictures of Al Ain (pages 8/9, 84/85, all on 86/87/88/89, 92/93 & 114/115, 104/105, 108/109, & 15, 82, 83, 112, 113, 119, inset); the photograph on the half title page of His Highness Sheikh Zayed and his sons was taken by Mr Zubara, the personal photographer to H.H. Sheikh Zayed. Some of the sons of H.H. Sheikh Zayed could not be present at the original

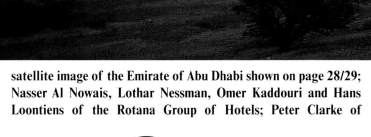

photo shoot and were added digitally by Omid Yazdani and Payam Rowhani of Gulf Colour Film Photography; Marycke Jongbloed; Katja Otter; Roger Le Meister (page 50/51); Mike Curtis (page 86 inset); Lucia Farah and the WAM archives of Abu Dhabi (pages 2, 3, 10/11, 54/55, 76/77, 90/91, 98/99, 110/111, & insets 12, 13, 14, 16, 19, 20, 22).

Our thanks to the following companies whose support and encouragement made the publication of this book possible; Lawrence Holliday, Rudy Chandler and William Saltzer of Abu Dhabi Ship Building; Abdullah Saleh, Walter Bailey and Bob Howard of Ducab; Mike Daly, Nick Cochrane-Dyet, Jeremy Bowen, Tim Bingham, Rick Capoccia and Barbara Patrick of British Petroleum; David Wild, Rod Ellis and Arafat Ali Khan of DHL; Jim Shuppert of General Electric; Wyche Bonnot of Emirates Commercial Business Services; Dr. Tayeb Kamali, John Metzner, Karen Ratcliffe and especially Lynn Nicks McCaleb of the Higher Colleges of Technology; Dick Marsten of NRSC, the National Remote Sensing Centre of the Centre of Excellence for Applied Research and Training in Abu Dhabi for the satellite image of the Emirate of Abu Dhabi shown on page 28/29; Nasser Al Nowais, Lothar Nessman, Omer Kaddouri and Hans Loontiens of the Rotana Group of Hotels; Peter Clarke of

Antoine Murad and especially, last but certainly not least, Fadi Sarkis of the National Bank of Abu Dhabi.

On a more personal note, we would like to express our gratitude to the following people, who continue to make a daily impact on our lives, for their support, encouragement and patience: Robert & Simone for their continuous support here in Dubai, our friend Fred Secca-Blagg, my son Marc and my mother, Marjorie, for looking after the UK book distribution, Kerri for graduating from Sam Houston University with her Masters in Educational Psychology, hearing impaired Nicholas, now **21**, who ably looks after the distribution of books in the USA, William, just **14** and six feet tall, for helping me with my computer, Lucy and Sally in York for being such fun and finally, to John, whose optimism and inspiration continues to cause exasperation to us all.

Thanks to you all.

GAMCO; Philip Michel, Bob Conover, John Doman and Phil Gaffney of the Cessna Aircraft Company; Mr Hisham Al-Sayed Al Hashemi & John Halaby of Gulf Business Foundation; and finally,

Christine C. Nowell & Nick Crawley,
Abu Dhabi, 2001.

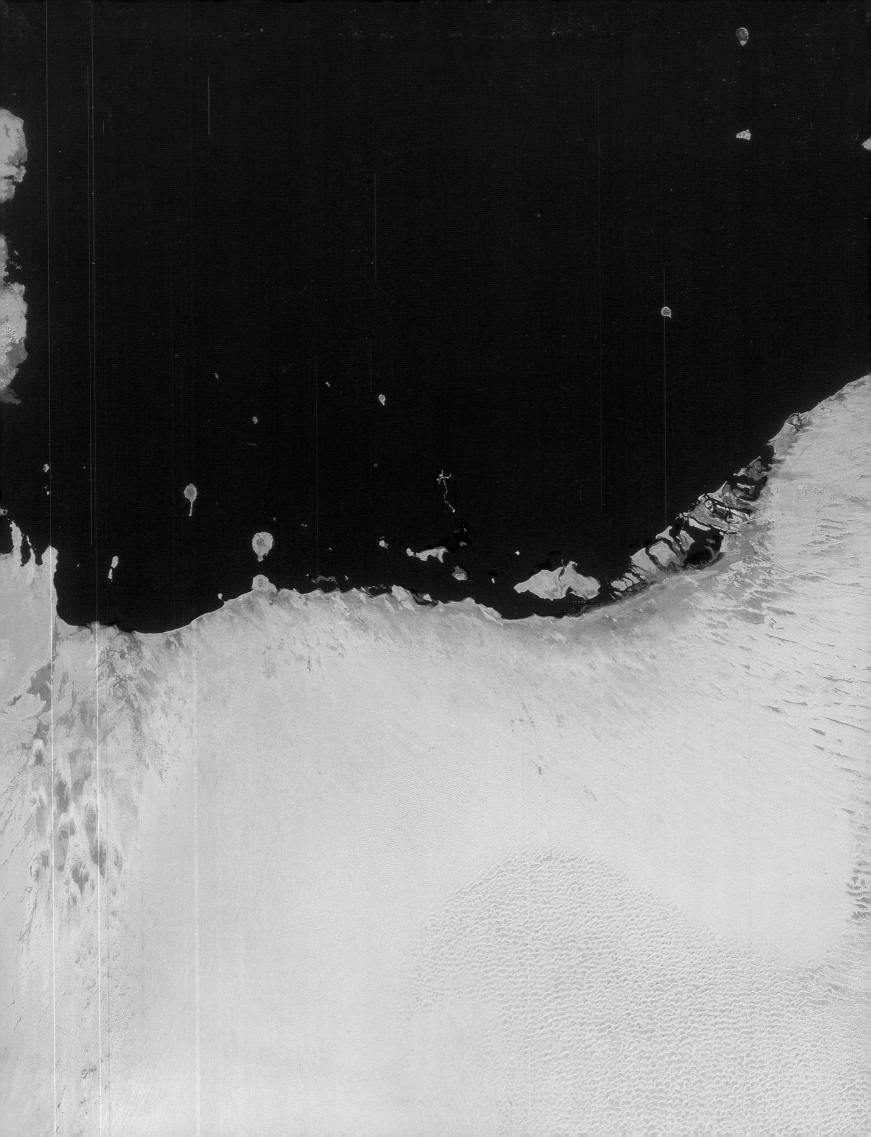